RAISING MEN NOT BOYS: DAILY AFFIRMATIONS TO UPLIFT YOUR SON

MARIA LEWIS RAMADANE, M.ED

WWW.TOTALLEARNINGSOLUTIONSCONSULTING.COM

RAISING MEN NOT BOYS: DAILY AFFIRMATIONS TO UPLIFT YOUR SON

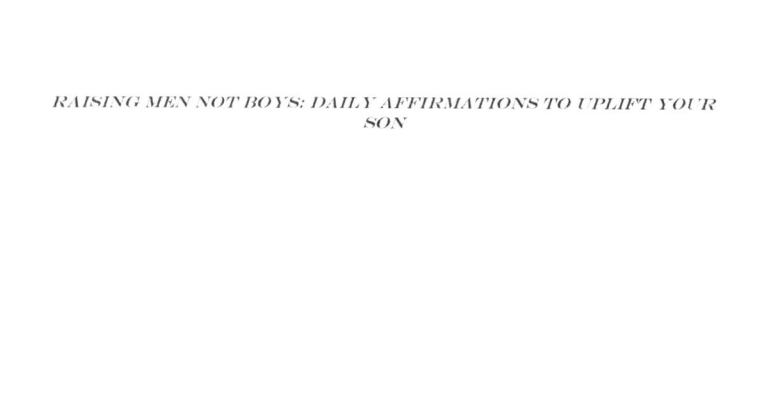

Copyright © 2017 TOTAL LEARNING SOLUTIONS CONSULTING GROUP, INC

All rights reserved. No part of this book may be reproduced or transmitted in any form or by any means, electronic or mechanical, including photocopying, recording, or by any information storage and retrieval system, without permission in writing from the copyright owner.

ISBN: 978-0692869277

Library of Congress Control Number: 2017905276

TOTAL LEARNING SOLUTIONS CONSULTING GROUP, INC SPOTSYLVANIA, VA

WWW.TOTALLEARNINGSOLUTIONSCONSULTING.COM

DEDICATION

THIS BOOK IS DEDICATED TO THE MOST PERFECT GIFTS THAT GOD GAVE ME. MY CHILDREN, MY YOUNG MEN, MY HEART; MALIK AND ISAIAH. I HAVE TAUGHT YOU LIFE LESSONS; BUT YOU TAUGHT ME LOVE LESSONS. I LEARNED UNCONDITIONAL LOVE. I LEARNED TO LISTEN MORE AND TALK LESS. YOU TAUGHT ME TO SEE THE "RAINBOW IN MY CLOUD." MY JOB AS YOUR MOTHER IS TO POUR LOVE, WISDOM, AND CONFIDENCE INTO YOU, SO THAT YOU CAN WALK IN YOUR PURPOSE. THE WORLD NEEDS YOU AND THE WORLD IS WAITING FOR YOU. EXTEND YOUR WINGS AND FLY.

"EVERYTHING IN LIFE COMES WITH A PRICE; KEEP INVESTING IN YOUR <u>OWN</u> ACCOUNT."

RAISING MEN NOT BOYS: DAILY AFFIRMATIONS TO UPLIFT YOUR SON

"YOU WERE BORN INTO GREATNESS. YOU HAVE ALL YOU NEED TO ACCOMPLISH YOUR GOALS."

WWW.TOTALLEARNINGSOLUTIONSCONSULTING.COM

"PICK FRIENDS THAT PUSH OR PULL YOU FORWARD. DON'T LET ANYONE HOLD YOU BACK."

RAISING MEN NOT BOYS: DAILY AFFIRMATIONS TO UPLIFT YOUR SON

"IF YOU REALLY WANT IT, DON'T STOP UNTIL YOU ACHIEVE IT."

WWW.TOTALLEARNINGSOLUTIONSCONSULTING.COM

"WHEN OBSTACLES ARE IN YOUR PATH, JUMP OVER THEM. LEARN THE LESSON AND DON'T LOOK BACK."

RAISING MEN NOT BOYS: DAILY AFFIRMATIONS TO UPLIFT YOUR SON

"WHAT GOD PUT IN YOU, NO ONE CAN TAKE AWAY FROM YOU."

WWW.TOTALLEARNINGSOLUTIONSCONSULTING.COM

"IF YOU BELIEVE IT; YOU CAN ACHIEVE IT. YOU DECIDE."

"GET UP, GET READY, AND FACE THE WORLD WITH CONFIDENCE."

RAISING MEN NOT BOYS: DAILY AFFIRMATIONS TO UPLIFT YOUR SON

"YOU ARE ROYALTY, WEAR YOUR CROWN WITH PRIDE."

WWW.TOTALLEARNINGSOLUTIONSCONSULTING.COM

"MAKE EACH MOMENT COUNT BECAUSE YOU NEVER GET TIME BACK."

"TALENT IS GOD GIVEN; HARD WORK IS YOUR CHOICE."

"DETERMINE YOUR MISSION AND LET YOUR MISSION DETERMINE YOUR ACTIONS."

"BE YOU; YOU ARE THE BEST AT IT!"

> "PREPARE YOURSELF BY DOING THE LITTLE THINGS. EVENTUALLY IT WILL ALL ADD UP."

"ALWAYS BE PREPARED TO WALK INTO AN OPPORTUNITY."

"ORGANIZE YOUR MIND; NARROW YOUR FOCUS AND SEE THE FINISH LINE."

"DON'T DROP THE FOOTBALL IN THE END ZONE; YOU DESERVE TO CROSS THAT LINE."

"NEVER BE SATISFIED; KEEP PUSHING YOURSELF. CELEBRATE BUT KEEP MOVING FORWARD."

WWW.TOTALLEARNINGSOLUTIONSCONSULTING.COM

"SEE THE VISION; ONCE YOU SEE IT, YOU CAN BE IT."

"LEAD WITH YOUR ACTIONS AND NOT JUST YOUR WORDS."

"STRENGTH IS NOT ONLY PHYSICAL, REAL STRENGTH IS DEVELOPED FROM WITHIN."

"SOMETIMES YOU NEED TO GO THROUGH A CHALLENGE TO GROW INTO YOUR SUCCESS."

RAISING MEN NOT BOYS: DAILY AFFIRMATIONS TO UPLIFT YOUR SON

"YOU ARE THE AUTHOR OF YOUR LIFE'S STORY; YOU CAN ALWAYS CHANGE THE STORYLINE."

WWW.TOTALLEARNINGSOLUTIONSCONSULTING.COM

> "DISCOVER YOUR PURPOSE AND ALLOW YOUR PURPOSE TO DIRECT YOUR PATH."

WWW.TOTALLEARNINGSOLUTIONSCONSULTING.COM

"DON'T WEAR A MASK THROUGH LIFE. TAKE IT OFF BECAUSE YOU ARE AMAZING."

"SHOW UP FOR YOURSELF EVERY DAY BECAUSE YOU ARE WORTH IT."

RAISING MEN NOT BOYS: DAILY AFFIRMATIONS TO UPLIFT YOUR SON

"YOU WILL FALL DOWN MILLIONS OF TIMES IN LIFE. NEVER GET TIRED OF STANDING BACK UP."

WWW.TOTALLEARNINGSOLUTIONSCONSULTING.COM

RAISING MEN NOT BOYS: DAILY AFFIRMATIONS TO UPLIFT YOUR SON

"GET RID OF ALL OF YOUR EXCUSES. YOU DON'T HAVE TIME TO MAKE THEM."

WWW.TOTALLEARNINGSOLUTIONSCONSULTING.COM

RAISING MEN NOT BOYS: DAILY AFFIRMATIONS TO UPLIFT YOUR SON

"HAPPINESS IS A DECISION. DON'T LET ANYONE DECIDE FOR YOU."

WWW.TOTALLEARNINGSOLUTIONSCONSULTING.COM

"STOP COMPARING YOURSELF TO OTHERS; NO ONE ELSE CAN BE BETTER AT BEING YOU THAN YOU."

RAISING MEN NOT BOYS: DAILY AFFIRMATIONS TO UPLIFT YOUR SON

"YOUR WORTH DOES NOT COME FROM OTHERS. YOUR WORTH AND VALUE IS A BIRTH RIGHT."

WWW.TOTALLEARNINGSOLUTIONSCONSULTING.COM

"YOU DON'T ALWAYS NEED APPLAUDS AND RECOGNITION FROM OTHERS. GIVE YOURSELF A STANDING OVATION."

"BE STRONG, BE HAPPY, AND BE KIND. YOU ARE AMAZING ALL BY YOURSELF."

"ALWAYS GO THE EXTRA MILE BECAUSE YOU NEVER KNOW WHAT IS WAITING BEYOND THE FINISH LINE."

"SLOW DOWN FOR A MOMENT BUT NEVER STOP PURSUING YOUR GOALS."

RAISING MEN NOT BOYS: DAILY AFFIRMATIONS TO UPLIFT YOUR SON

"YOU ARE NOT PERFECT. IF YOU MAKE A MISTAKE, FORGIVE YOURSELF. LET IT GO AND KEEP RUNNING YOUR RACE."

WWW.TOTALLEARNINGSOLUTIONSCONSULTING.COM

"FAILURE ONLY MEANS THAT YOU HAVE AN OPPORTUNITY TO TRY AGAIN."

"DON'T WASTE YOUR LIFE BY SITTING ON THE SIDELINE, GET IN THE GAME AND GIVE IT YOUR ALL."

"WHEN SOMEONE THROWS YOU THE BALL, YOU DECIDE THE NEXT MOVE."

"EDUCATION OPENS THE DOOR BUT ONLY YOU CAN DECIDE YOUR NEXT STEP."

"WHEN YOU NEED ENCOURAGEMENT, LOOK WITHIN. YOU WERE MADE FOR GREATNESS."

"RESPECT STARTS ON THE INSIDE."

> "LOVE YOURSELF. BECAUSE YOU ARE EXTRAORDINARY. DON'T PLAY SMALL."

RAISING MEN NOT BOYS: DAILY AFFIRMATIONS TO UPLIFT YOUR SON

"YOU DON'T HAVE TO BE EVERYTHING TO EVERYBODY. A TRUE FRIEND WILL GIVE YOU AS MUCH AS YOU GIVE THEM."

WWW.TOTALLEARNINGSOLUTIONSCONSULTING.COM

"DON'T GUARD YOUR HEART. LOVE FREELY."

RAISING MEN NOT BOYS: DAILY AFFIRMATIONS TO UPLIFT YOUR SON

"IF YOU CAN'T BELIEVE IN YOURSELF JUST YET, USE MY BELIEF IN YOU TO PROPEL YOURSELF FORWARD."

WWW.TOTALLEARNINGSOLUTIONSCONSULTING.COM

"ONE OPPORTUNITY CAN SHIFT THE COURSE OF YOUR JOURNEY."

"DON'T GIVE ANYONE ELSE THE KEYS TO YOUR LIFE. YOU ARE THE ONE IN CONTROL. ALWAYS STAY BEHIND THE WHEEL."

"THE ENERGY THAT SURROUNDS YOU GIVES LIFE TO OTHERS; KEEP IT POSITIVE."

"DON'T RELY ON WHAT YOU SEE TODAY BECAUSE YOU ARE ONLY STEPS AWAY FROM AN AMAZING TOMORROW."

"EVERYONE IS NOT GOING TO BE ON YOUR TEAM. YOUR OPPONENTS ARE THERE TO HELP BUILD YOUR CHARACTER."

RAISING MEN NOT BOYS: DAILY AFFIRMATIONS TO UPLIFT YOUR SON

"DON'T LET FEAR STEAL YOUR SUCCESS."

WWW.TOTALLEARNINGSOLUTIONSCONSULTING.COM

RAISING MEN NOT BOYS: DAILY AFFIRMATIONS TO UPLIFT YOUR SON

"EVERY DAY IS AN OPPORTUNITY TO BE YOUR BEST. BE YOUR BEST TODAY."

WWW.TOTALLEARNINGSOLUTIONSCONSULTING.COM

"YOUR CIRCLE OF FRIENDS MUST BE MOVING IN THE SAME DIRECTION AS YOU, OR YOU WILL COLLIDE."

RAISING MEN NOT BOYS: DAILY AFFIRMATIONS TO UPLIFT YOUR SON

"AS THE SAYING GOES, 'IF YOU BELIEVE IT, YOU CAN ACHIEVE IT.' YOU DECIDE."

WWW.TOTALLEARNINGSOLUTIONSCONSULTING.COM

CONTACT INFORMATION

TLS Consulting Inc

P.O. Box 511

Spotsylvania, VA 22553-9998

www.TotalLearningSolutionsConsulting.com

mramadane@TotalLearningSolutionsconsulting.com

Facebook: @TotalLearningSolutionsconsulting

Instagram: @TLSconsulting

Made in the USA
Monee, IL
16 March 2024